Tethered Thoughts

Stephanie Perry and Tanya
Lakin

BookLeaf
Publishing
India | USA | UK

Tethered Thoughts is dedicated to anyone who has ever felt adrift. It honors the thoughts that make us up and make us who we are. As we get older, thoughts that tethered us can either stay or fade. This book is our thoughts that once threaded through us, laid out unapologetically.

ACKNOWLEDGEMENT

To all the high and lows, the loves lost, the loves found, to all the footprints that crossed our souls and made their mark, for better or for worse, this is our story.

PREFACE

Our poems come from intimate thoughts and reflections that we have had throughout our lives. They are our subconscious, our conscious, and our inner thoughts that have fought self righteously for their place.

Unraveling

I speak from a place of faint consciousness
My unconscious rewarding my innate reactions
to actions
Caught in a cycle
It's hard to counteract
To think independent thoughts
Is it merely a myth?
Searching my consciousness for blind spots
I implore them to wake
Reshape
Lured by scripts of my subculture
Inspecting its structure, looking for the cracks
Prying open the things people told me that I
thought were facts
Everything is fiction
Driven by my ego addiction
I want to touch everything and for it not to be
real
I want to sink into the pages of a book
Learn facts and ideas to counteract my
conditioning
Tinkered by society
All these notions ingrained
Seeking to break up this interconnected chain
Life can be different if we peer close

Evolving to be more than the sum of the parts
we were given
I will pick
Until I unravel
Until I am bits and pieces
Parts of me
It's a pursuit
To come undone
Searching to put oneself together
So one doesn't feel so numb

Father Father

Look at me father
Bereft from you
Years pass and things stay the same
Things unsaid
Times unspent
Times spent
Leaves stains under the flesh

See me father, over here
Is enough of me, enough for you

Tell me
Am I
Could I
Will I
Am I

The syrup of you
Negates me
Pounding thoughts
Pollutes me
Serrated thoughts
Slice me
Pounding thoughts …
Look at me father

Your rationed love
Eats at the flesh binding me
Penetrates anxieties manifesting the disdain of
me
Weakens me with reaching hands
Retch the bile of me
Regurgitate a multi-coloured mess of me

See me father, over here
Is enough of me, enough for you

Am I
Do you
Am I
Could you
Will you
Am I

It's been a long while, father
The child I was, laid with weighted dreams
Upon a pillow of still memories
The child I was, whispered prays for you, you of
yesterday
To have loved me in my yesterdays
The child I was, prayed in silence with clasped
hands at the dead of night for your return
The child I was, filled with the loss of you
An appetite of wanting fed my desires
Weakened me with reaching hands

Purging the loss of you until I saw the bile of me
Regurgitated, a multi-coloured mess of me

Look at me father
Your presence an echo
Ebbing away
Nothing to cling to but the blood of me
Resuscitate me
Holding myself in contempt
The yolk of me bleeds my conscience immoral
Seeking my restitution of self, in the love of me,
from you
See me father, over here
Twinned in you, running through you
Away from you
Look at me father
Look at me father
Look at me father
See me father, over here
You're the neurosis in me
Contaminated with hurt
Wanting you
Hating me
Unsaid things
Call out to me
Hating on you
Waiting on you
Weakened me with reaching hands
Slicing the loss of you from me

Drain the blood of you, from me
A mess of me
See me father, over here
Is this enough for you

Look at me father
See me father, over here
Look at me father
This is for you

The Chalice

You picked apart the threads that sewed her up
Laced the strings to your hands
A puppet master with some grand plan
You filled her up with your lies
Interlaced them with cyanide
Trying to kill her spirit and take her drive
You wore her down till her bones began to crush
To leave all but dust
But as her will ebbed
She garnered her strength
To reject his poisoned chalice
As there comes a point when a woman's throat
closes up
His toxic words
Slung from his tongue can't be undone
They lay forever in her mind
Weakened by his words
Once a vessel
Now a broken bird
But she rises
Just enough
To fight
To strive
To live
What we must know

Is even as a man tries to kill a woman with
words like swords
She'll rise above what he told her she was
Because to be a woman means to fight and strive
Against the mighty man who holds misogyny
under smiling eyes

Rabbit Hole

When the engines stop
And I hear no roar
When the fire stops outside my door
When the rumble settles
When the mess of the thoughts in my head
Take a moment to rest
I land on a safety strip
Where I can grasp the words and sounds I seek
That thing called clarity But safety doesn't feel
so safe
As my past turmoil climbs upon my raft
 Its heavy weight begins to make me sink
The past isn't my friend
But a place for my sanity to leak
And as I grasp for landI don't know where to
stand
Security is a trapdoor
Safety is a battlefield
My past comes to haunt
You could be happy
And it smiles
Winks
And down the rabbit hole you sink

FINE

I'm fine
I'm fine
I'm fine
Said the girl to anyone who would pretend to
listen
As tears spoiled her eyes

I'm fine
I'm fine
I'm fine
Reaching out but staying hidden
She searches their face for recognition

I'm fine
I'm fine
I'm fine
It isn't what is said, but how it is said
Her words lose shape
Stay unspoken

I'm fine
I'm fine
I'm fine
Can they see this heart that's so very bruised
Begging to be noticed

But, leave me alone

I'm fine
I'm fine
I'm fine
Somehow, I feel bereaved

I'm fine
I'm fine
I'm fine
You seem to care but your eyes tell a different
story
I need you to stand further over there

I'm fine
I'm fine
I'm fine
I don't need you
I barely need me
Maybe not needing someone for so long has
made me feel bereaved

I'm fine
I'm fine
I'm fine
Why would I say more to you when you aren't
even there
I'm not even here

I'm fine
I'm fine
I'm fine
Protection is costly
Yet, a comfort

I'm fine
I'm fine
I'm fine
Does our emotional state somehow make us bad

I'm fine
I'm fine
I'm fine
I think I might be emotionally spent

13 Reasons Why

I see that fire in your eyes, that desire as you
look at my parts, the bits, the items of me
Like a shopping list
Tick, tick, tick
And I can see you thinking
"That's not me, one of the guys on her 13
reasons why."
But take a look at yourself,
Take a look inside

I see you as you smile and lean over and wink
And say do you want to go back to mine after
this drink,
I smile and say yes, we fuck, and we undress
Then I don't hear from you again
You've decided I'm easy
That kind of girl
Not the one you take home to your mum or put a
ring on their hand
You've decided I'm that kinda girl
The one night stand
And I can see you thinking,
"That's not me, one of the guys on her 13
reasons why"
But I see your double standards,
Now you should take a look inside

I see you as you
Swipe, swipe, swipe
Like an addict, like it's crack
You are swiping in vain, in vain, in vain
You say
'Hey I'm here for a good time not a long time'
'Hey, fancy a fuck'
'Hey, I like busty girls, what cup size are you?'
'Hey I like a big ass, do you squat too'
We are a fast food generation
Tick, tick , tick
Waiting for our next quick fix
And I can see you thinking,
"That's not me, one of the guys on her 13
reasons why",
But take a look at yourself,
Take a look inside

I see you
Your wandering gaze
Thinking I should be flattered you looked my
way
But as your eyes fall upon my body all I feel is
disgust
Like my body was only built for your unbridled
lust
Lust is power and soon turns sour
One day you won't look at me the same

I won't be shiny and new
You'll think our love has changed
But maybe it's just because
We don't fuck like we used to
Then your eyes wander and find a new body
Maybe this is natural
Maybe this is true
But if you choose monogamy
Try a little harder to love me like you promised
to

I see you as you treat me like the shows you
watch
Porn hub
Red tube
Spit, Slap
Call you Daddy
Call me whore
Treat me like the woman on all fours
I'm not a porn star
But you think that's how it's done
You've been watching too much porn and now
it's not just for fun
It's in the way you hold my neck, a vice too tight
in bed
I want to make love as you tell me you'll fuck
me proper hard tonight
What happened to sex?
Too many people on the internet

Not laying next to each other trying to connect
And I can see you thinking, "That's not me, one
the guys on her 13 reasons why"
But take a look at yourself,
Take a look inside

I see you
The cat calls and the jeers
But that happens to women all the time
From the building sites
The white vans
To the people on Instagram
The way you make lists of what's hot, what's
not, what's in and what's out
A shopping list
That's where we found ourselves again,
Tick, tick tick
And I can see you thinking, "That's not me, one
the guys on her 13 reasons why"
But take a look at yourself,
Take a look inside

I see you
The man in the office who guffaws Macho as he
laughs #metoo
What's all this aggro for
Men can't be men anymore
Women are too defensive
Too sensitive

We take things to heart
He's just flirting as he slaps your arse
He's just flirting
It's just banter
Then he puffs his chest and talks to you in that
way
That he would never
To any male colleague any day
I'm not sensitive
I've just had enough
So if you can't tell, I'm not flirting with you
I'll file you under
Men I've had enough of
And I can see you thinking, "That's not me, one
of the guys on her 13 reasons why"
But take a look at yourself,
Take a look from inside

I see you
The man who thinks he's enlightened
But stills wants you to be a certain girl
A certain way
Confident but not too shy
Loud but not too loud
He wants you to be one of the boys but not too
much
He wants you to have an opinion but know when
to shut up

He wants the cool girl, but he wants her when he
wants her
To bring her out like a dancing doll
And I can see you thinking, "That's not me, one
of the guys on her 13 reasons why"
But take a look at yourself,
Take a look inside

I see you
The man who surprises me with his guise
The gentleman persona
As he lays his trap
Me none the wiser
Then when he's got me
His mind wanders
It really was all about the chase
What do you do with a girl when the chase is
done? Case closed, next one
And I can see you thinking, "That's not me, one
of the guys on her 13 reasons why"
But take a look at yourself,
Take a look inside

I see you
The man who treats me like a prop
Here just to be the girl you get in and out of the
box
I'm a weekend investment
When the boys aren't out to play

I think you see me as a commodity
Something to trade
Then when I'm too drunk to know where I am
You pass me around to your best friend Sam
But you were sharing and that's ok, because
boys will be boys and I probably deserved it
anyway
And I can see you thinking, "That's not me, one
of the guys on her 13 reasons why"
But take a look at yourself,
Take a look inside

I see you
The man who doesn't take no for an answer
You sat next to me
On the bus
On the the tube
Maybe you stopped me in the street
And I'm trying not to be rude
I said no, but you kept asking anyway
No once
Twice
Is he listening
So just to be clear
Just so you know
I'm not being shy
And being persistent isn't romantic
It's called harassment and that's it, you know it

But you'll call me moody and tell me not to be
such a bitch
Maybe I'm a lesbian or a crazy feminist
or
Maybe I'm just fed up of saying no and nobody
is bloody hearing it
And I can see you thinking, "That's not me, one
of the guys on her 13 reasons why"
But take a look at yourself,
Take a look inside

I see you all
Thinking fuck me
She's cynical
But the next two are the worst to come
These are the reasons I think I've become
undone
I think I'm one of you, one of them
Sitting here objectifying
Men
Eyes, Abs, Ass
One night's enough
Nothing lasts
Desire, lust
That's it
That's all
Expectations fall
Swipe, swipe, swipe
Tick, tick, tick

If he's not 6ft 3
I mean, forget it
Oh fuck, oh God
My ideals are starting to rot
I mean
This whole dating scene seems obscene
Where have all the good men gone
But, No.13
Maybe this is the worst of all
When you can't tell who's good at all
You laugh at the
Fairy tales peddled by Disney and Hollywood
It's just a dream from childhood
Then he takes you by the hand
And you think I've seen you all before
Carbon copies
1, 2, 3, 4
He winces
Flinches
Turns away
I say
Are you a coward?
Am I too broken to be of any good
And I ask
Where have all the good men gone
Where are all the gods
Where's the streetwise Hercules to fight the
rising odds
And I call you a coward

You turn away
This broken heart is too much for you to stay

22

This Little Heart of Mine

23

There's that moment in time
Where someone catches you off guard

A moment in time they slip past the shadows
That echo in your heart

They dust and shine and bring anew
This little heart that once felt so blue

Firestarter

24

Your kisses touch my lips
My body feels every part of it
Your kisses are gentle and strong
Always knowing what my body wants
There's a fire that you've lit
And all my thoughts are all consumed by it

You're a firestarter
Burning down the walls
Petrol ignited as I free fall
As I spend hours thinking of all the things you
do
Consumed to be consumed by you

You're a firestarter
And I can feel the pulse of you
Embers and cinders
Engulf into a magnitude of dancing flames
Lust here has no shame

You're a firestarter
As you touch my skin
And it lets your energy in
The fire simmers, burns
Rages in places unheard

You're a firestarter
Turning up the heat
Eyes burning
Loins turning
An inside guttural yearning

You're my firestarter
Come kiss me now
Come burn bright
Firestarter stay with me
Let's start to discover places no one's been

MeToo

The world is crumbling and you've been looking
at your feet
Wondering if you'll say
Me Too
Wondering if it's time to admit out loud the
things you blamed on yourself

The memories like razors blades
That dance like whisky in your veins
And play like music on fade

I apologised when you came onto me
I pushed you away, but
I must have asked for it because I was smiling
your way

Bruises on my shoulders and bruises in my heart
Maybe after all, I am tart

I apologised when you invited me to sit at the
head table like some prize
You put your hand on my leg and slid it up my
thigh
I said sorry, I think I want to sit with my friends
tonight

Bruises on my thigh and in my heart
Maybe after all, I am a tart

I apologised when I was too drunk to see
When you got into bed nonconsensually

Bruises on my body and bruises in my heart
Maybe after all, I am a tart

I apologised when I said no and you said yes
I went quiet and you just went ahead
Why couldn't I say no
When you just took what you thought you were
owed

Bruises on my body and bruises in my heart
Maybe after all I am a tart

Memories are like razor blades
That dance like whisky in my veins
And play like music on fade

I look back at the things I didn't say
A strangled voice
An echo of
Boys will be boys
Until they're men
And all I ask is, what then?

Memories are like razor blades
That dance like whisky in my veins
And play like music on fade

Tiny Dancer

Sometimes I feel like a clown
Or a juggler in a maze
Sometimes I feel like a dancer
Just trying to make my way
Sometimes I feel like a magician
Learning new tricks
Sometimes I'm a comedian looking for some
laughter to give me validated kicks
Sometimes I'm an actor
Pretending
Or a musician with a score
Sometimes I'm just a puppet to the master on the
days my ego is sore
I'm just the entertainer
Finding ways to entertain
Sometimes I'm just a dancer
And it feels like I'm dancing in the rain

Tonight

I see the mum as she clasps her hands with fear,
I see the dad as he holds back the tears,
I see the kid who cries,
The teenager who's mute,
I see the wounds,
Not on the outside but the inside too,
And the inside wounds,
They are the worst,
The wounds like puncture marks,
Unerasable scars,
I see the doctors as they give bad news,
I see the nurse as they write their notes,
Tired, bleary eyed,
Wondering if they'll get home to their family
before they go to bed tonight,
I see the student crying,
Worried,
Wondering if they're up for the job,
I see the chaplain as he kneels to pray,
As he whispers that this child will go to heaven
today,
I see the baby,
Too young to fend,
The infant unsteady on their feet,
I see the teenager too tired for their years,
I see all the people,

All the time,
Fighting for their lives,
And tonight,
I see the sisters, the brothers,
The aunts, the uncles, the cousins and more,
As they look over at their family laid in bed
praying for more,
For more time,
I see the worry in their furrowed brow,
I see them pray to a god they said
Wasn't there,
Isn't true
But now to anything they pray,
Just to pull them through,
I see the hope,
I see the despair,
I see it all,
Even the unsaid words hanging in the air,
I see the mother as she bends to kiss her child's
cheek for their last moment of bliss,
I see the arduous pain flit through her eyes,
Knowing tonight,
A life might be different,
A life might be halved,
And as she lifts her head to close her eyes,
She whispers words of comfort for one last time.

Violated Beauty

You ask me to dig myself up
Lay my petals down for worship
To love the depths of their colour
Their form
To seek appreciation
Yet society never taught me to love the skin I
live within
It taught me hate and fear
Afflicted by my reflection
With hateful spin
Thoughts rapidly gather
Expanding my skin
The air surrounding me thickens
Thoughts create holes in my common sense
I admonish my will
I violated myself
The demigod of beauty
Preaches to me
Scolds my form
Visions of what we are told to be
Flicker
Flinch
Hide
Fight
Woman is a creature
I feel unsafe within

Noir

The sky withdraws its blue
A deluge of noir
Unfurls an appetite
Of sorrow
Warming her with melancholy
Bleakness amasses
In her furrowed charcoal eyes
Locking in an overwhelming arousal of
monochromatic feelings
Uncompromising delusions accumulate
Weaponizing her thoughts
Coveting domination
Dissenting voices collide
Into a constellation of interlocking
Disorienting perceptions
Sensitizing her sanity
Fusing futility
In her
Defence seems futile
Hypnotized with inaction
Maladaptive attunement
Seeks devout streams of volatile consciousness
She's unable to reject
Succumbing to a distorted reality
Not wanting to lose herself in the air
She wishes she wasn't so loud in quiet places

Silence is the enemy that courts her
Her mind battles thoughts
Dispelling harmony
Circulating and catching
Holding her in a state of noir

Trinket of Love

I lay nestled here
Ornate
Dainty
Held close
Handled by your delicate touch
Cupped by your careful hands
You lay me down with care

I feel your pride as you trace my design
Your gaze tells me of my beauty
A visual ecstasy to you
Like precious gold
You shield me with guard

Holding me too tight
In your hands
Handled for too long
I beg you not to handle me with
Such considered attention
For frequent acquaintances breeds contempt

Your eyes trace my design unpicking my beauty
Peering too close
Your gaze holds me too long
Like a treasured prize
Tarnished from your locked-in embrace

My glory begins to fade
My cracks appear like apparitions to you
Carelessly forgetting
Trying to fix me
Restoring the beauty you once had seen

Can you not just hold me
In time
Without forgetting
Once you thought of me as precious gold
Cupped in your hands
You once protected me
Now shielding me from you
I lay cold
From your touch

Blue Them

37

The sky's blue has been imbued
Into me
Blue thoughts
Anchor my veins
Dragging at my feet

Dirty Rules

Dirty rules
Govern policies that
Hear voices with
Pens poised
With preconceived
Opinions
Guarding laws
Paternalistically
Repressive
Scalding all that
Aren't the norm
Normative ideals
Crystallize policies
Dehumanizing
Identities
Repressing
Diversity
For nothing
But fragile egos

Awaken

Do you ever feel you lose your grip
And reality warps regressively
Implicit manifestations
Succeed
Blinded with inaction
In action
Your bones awaken with memories and performs
rituals
Repeating on a loop
Reality secedes
Embodying you with someone
Other than you

Futile

It's the weight of hopelessness
It's the mundane
It's the hours filled with repetition
That flow fast and slow
It's the limitations of living
Which bears it's presence upon my pull
So all I am is my will
That struggles in its decline

Walls

Unforeseen, I lay
Fortified within flesh and bone
The chambers of my heart have thickened
Built itself a fortress
Beating within my ribs
Fighting fracture

Femininity Sells

42

Femininity sits on the tongues of men
They speak of a warped vision of how women
should be
They regurgitate the rules fed to them
Magazines offering up women's daily rituals
How to act
What to wear
How to look
Too little
Too much
Either end we bear the cross
Shamed for effort
Shamed for not enough
Trying to sink in to the narratives sold to us
We rebel
Or comply
They tell us
You are too old
Too fat
Too thin
Society demands us
To buy this
To buy that
You'll be happy when you aren't fat
Consumerism sells femininity
Magazines, papers, posters on the tube

They wrap it up and present it like a gift
They sell
We buy
They scream
Exercise until you're lean
The ads offer up youth
Botox, facelifts, expensive creams
Until people point and call us obscene
Shamed if we do, shamed if we don't
Femininity has its rules
A sell by date
When I was younger I stuck chicken fillets in
my bra cups and dieted so I could be sexy
enough to fuck
I shaved my legs and plucked my eyebrows
I was ashamed of my vagina between my thighs
But as I get older I begin to disregard
All the things I was sold and told to be
It's a horrid subjection
To which I have an objection
Femininity
The words sit on my tongue
How to be a woman
The magazine article calls
A quiz
'How to be sexy'
'How to get a guy'
An algorithm of fabricated lies
That tell us

To tug and pull
To inject and wax
To shave and paint
To tan and dye
To tell our lovers a lie
Oh, how to be a woman
Lots of people tell
You're a prize if you're pretty enough
Get fillers in your lips
Stop the aging process
Because if you're old you ain't fit
Too much
Too little
Either end we bear the cross
Shamed for effort
Shamed for not enough
Do this, do that
The magazines yell
From men behind their desk
Whisky in their hand
Porn hub in their browser
It's hard to shut the world out as it infiltrates
In trying to tell us not to be happy
When we can buy it
A simple cash transaction
For more satisfaction
Consumerism
Sell
Sell

Sell
A one way road to hell

45

Moment of Smiles

Once upon time
I remember a moment
Before the future took hold of the past
Where the laughter parted the corners of her lips
Ours
As we felt the floor slip between our feet
In circles we let ourselves be guided
Her hair was floating
Dreamlike
Her smile my prize
Nonsensical movements
Led us in circles
As songs parted our lips
And it was whimsical
Soft in focus
A water-color memory

9 789357 448758